FROM BONDAGE
TO FREEDOM

COMPILED BY
VINOKIA J. MOSES

Dedication

This book is dedicated to every woman who has ever felt stuck, silenced, or shattered.

To the girl who cried herself to sleep.

To the woman who smiled while breaking inside.

To the warrior who kept going when quitting felt easier. You are not forgotten. You are seen. And you are worth the fight for freedom.

Acknowledgments

To our Heavenly Father—thank You for being the Chain Breaker, the Way Maker, and the One who sees us even when we are hidden in the shadows. Every story in this book is a testimony of Your faithfulness.

To the powerful women who contributed to this work—thank you for your yes. Thank you for being brave enough to share your truth and vulnerable enough to let others heal through it. You are voices of freedom, and your courage has shifted atmospheres.

To every prayer warrior, supporter, and behind-the-scenes encourager —your intercession, and belief in this vision means more than words can express. This book would not exist without your unwavering support.

TABLE OF CONTENTS

Prophetess Sharon Allen

FREE!!

Free means not under the control or in the power of another, able to act or be done as one wishes.

Spiritual freedom to me is found in- *2 Corinthians 3:17 "Now the Lord is the Spirit, and where the Spirit of the Lord is, there is freedom." "And you will know the truth, and the truth will set you free."* "Live as people who are free, not using your freedom as a cover-up for evil, but living as servants of God."

That's powerful! We can't live a free life and use it as a cover-up for anything other than what God has instructed us to do. We talk with our lips, but our hearts are far from Him, from the freedom of bondage.

Can we ever be free from bondage? Can you truly break free? Can we be free from sin but living in bondage? I stated these questions to you because I first had to ask them to myself. Bondage is defined as the state of being bound. The state or practice of being physically restrained, such as by being tied up, chained, or put in handcuff. I don't know what your story is concerning bondage, but mine have been so real to the point I thought I would never be free. My bondage was the bondage within, and the struggles and fights from within my mind. The enemy was like a bombardier who released bombs. These bombs were illegal bombs invading my mind with thoughts contrary to the will of God for my life.

I didn't know early in my life what I know now, and that is that God was with me. These scriptures are what I live by to keep me from Bondage to Freedom.

To be free from bondage you must live a truthful life, and be honest about yourself. Not allowing yourself to be deceived about you. Open your heart to God and allow Him to shine His light of truth on the inside of you and acknowledge what has been revealed. Don't walk away and keep yourself entangled, *Galatians 5:1 (KJV) "Stand fast therefore in the liberty wherewith Christ has set us free, and not be entangled again with the yoke of bondage." "It is for freedom that Christ has set us free. Stand firm, then, and do not let yourselves be burdened again by a yoke of slavery." Galatians 5 (NIV)*

I say again, don't walk away from what the Spirit of God is revealing through His mirror. James 1:22-27 (MSG) Act on what you hear! Those who hear and don't act are like those who glance in the mirror, walk away, and two minutes later have no idea who they are, or what they look like. But whoever catches a glimpse of the revealed counsel of God - the free life

In God's revealing mirror, you can see where you need to make changes, and you can allow God to begin to realign your heart with His. James reveals the word of God is like a mirror, so when we read the Word of God, the Bible, it exposes what is really in our hearts. Our sins, our shortcomings, the areas of life where we need to repent and turn away from completely so that we can have freedom from any bondage.

Yes, many of us don't want to confront our issues or the bondage that keeps us so deceived about ourselves. But what's so great about when we do, God can do his wonderful work of transformation in our hearts. This is the beauty of God's word, the scriptures coming alive, being in my heart, it saved me! Learn to accept what Daddy God reveals to you, it will heal you and make you whole.

"Anyone who listens to the word but does not do what it says is like someone who looks at his face in a mirror and, after looking at himself, goes away and immediately forgets what he looks like" (James 1:23-24)

God truly wants us to come from bondage to freedom in him. He wants us to look like him, his son Christ Jesus each day of our life. Because of that, here is another powerful scripture that transformed my life:

Galatians 2:20 (AMP) "I have been crucified with Christ [that is, in Him I have shared his crucifixion]; it is no longer I who live, but Christ who lives in me." The life I now live in the body I live by faith [by adhering to, relying on, and completely trusting] in the son of God, who loved me and gave himself up for me."

This scripture is so powerful to me because I chose to die to me. I chose to see myself as Daddy God revealed it to me. I didn't want to live a deceitful life, but I knew in my heart if I listened to and saw what my Daddy God was showing me and began to work on me with his help, I would always be free. This scripture taught me to walk uprightly according to the truth of who I am in Christ Jesus. As he sacrificed himself for me, I sacrificed myself for Him. "It is no longer I who live but Christ who lives within me."

As we come from bondage to freedom, we must choose also to be free from every illegal thought. In my last book "Heart Check" I wrote as a child. I created an imaginary world where

I could escape the harsh reality of my life. My thoughts were a place where I won every battle. It was a place where I would think of ways of getting back at those who did me wrong. I had vain thoughts running rapidly through my mind. My thoughts were a playground for the enemy. Many people do not think anything is wrong with their thought patterns. But the bible tells us to take every thought captive when it doesn't give glory to God, His will and purpose for our life. 2 Corinthians 10:3-5 (KJV) says *"For though we walk in the flesh, we do not war after the flesh: ⁴(For the weapons of our warfare are not carnal, but mighty through God to the pulling down of strongholds;) 5Casting down imaginations, and every high thing that exalted itself against the knowledge of God, and bringing into captivity every thought to the obedience of Christ."*

Verse 5 in The Voice says, *"We are demolishing arguments and ideas, every high-and-mighty philosophy that puts itself against the knowledge of the one true God."* We are taking prisoners of every thought, every emotion, and subduing them into obedience to the Anointed One." I like how the Voice stated verse 5. It says it so clearly that a child can understand what the Father is saying to us concerning our thought life. There have been stronghold that keeps us in bondage and keeps us from being free, they have been erected in our minds, and therefore the Bible teaches us as believers that the way to have a renewed mind and to pull down strongholds is to bring "every thought into captivity to the obedience of Christ.

When we walk in obedience to Christ, we have our freedom from bondage.

The word obedience used in verse 5 of 2 Corinthians is *hupakoe*. It comes from *hupo*, meaning "under," as in under the rule of someone, to abide or remain. If we stay under the rule of Christ Jesus and abide in Him we will be free. The second half of the word *hupakoe* is *akouo* meaning "to hear." The word signifies attentive hearing, listening with compliance submission, assent, and agreement. It expresses hearing with a predisposition to obedience; a hearing to do. We bring our thoughts under the lordship of Christ. In other words, we obey God's word with our minds.

Bondage/strongholds can be as simple as having the false inner belief that God would not do the things that he has promised. I have been there. Will he? Can he? Deep within me

- those thoughts that question Him being all that He said He is to me. But I remained under his guidance, I kept on listening to his voice. Another point, any inner belief or thought that limits or blocks you from being what God created you to be is a stronghold. I want you to know that these strongholds or any kind of bondage can be pulled down by the power of the Holy Spirit and by renewing your mind with the word of God.

In closing, I remember during the years of raising my three children alone, I was in bondage in my mind, and I held on to a lot of strongholds during those years. But I desired to live a life dedicated to God. I'm free!!!

The final scripture that describes me coming from bondage to freedom is found in the book of Romans 12. The key to being sure you are free is to live a sacrificial life unto God. (The Voice) "Brothers and sisters, in light of all I have shared with you about God's mercies, I urge you to offer your bodies as a living and holy sacrifice to God, a sacred offering that pleases Him; this is your reasonable, essential worship. #2 - Do not allow this world to mold you to its image. Instead, be transformed from the inside out by renewing your mind. As a result, you will be able to discern what God's will and whatever God finds good, pleasing, and complete."

Paul urges those who read and hear his letter to respond to the good news by offering their bodies - eyes, ears, mouths, hands, feet-to God as a living sacrifice. Paul knows well enough that sacrifices end in death, not life. But the sacrifice of Jesus changes everything. His resurrection steals life from death and makes it possible for those who trust in him to become a sacrifice and yet live. But how do we live? We do not live as before, wrapping ourselves in the world and its bankrupt values. We live in constant renewal and transformation of our minds. Remember the scripture I gave to you earlier Galatians 2:20? *"It is no longer I who live but Christ who lives within me."* It is the truth of my life. All the scriptures I have stated in this story represent my life as it is today-FREE!!

Prayer of Freedom:

Lord, I come today with a heart full of hope and a mind filled with expectation for your Sons and Daughters who read this story. As You are with me every step of the way, be with them as they take their step of faith in surrendering all their bondage and strongholds to You. Let them not walk away from the mirror which is You speaking to them. But let them embrace it with a heart eager to be all You desire them to be, obeying you fully. Remain and abiding in You, listening with an intentional heart. Holy Spirit, I pray for them to long to walk in the full freedom that only You give. Break the chains of the law, sin, and addiction. Free them to live with joy and worship without restraint. Continue to guide our path and lead us toward a life of true freedom. Your word promises that where the spirit of the Lord is, there is freedom. Thank you, Daddy God, for helping us to come from bondage to freedom. Amen!!

Biography
Prophetess Sharon Allen

Prophetess Sharon Allen is a devoted follower of God, whom she affectionately refers to as Daddy God. She is an active member of Outpouring International Ministries, where she is under the leadership of Bishop Glenn and Apostle Shanita Jeffrey. In addition to her spiritual pursuits, Prophetess Sharon is a proud mother of three children and a grandmother to 8 and one on the way. Her role extends beyond her family, serving as a spiritual mentor and counselor to many individuals worldwide.

With over 30 years in ministry, Prophetess Allen is an ordained Prophetess of the Lord. She brings strong leadership to the church and has a heart for both local and global mission fields. Prophetess Sharon's passion is driven to advance the Kingdom of God by living her life according to Isaiah 61, Galatians 2:20, and Romans 12: 1- 2. Her heart's mission is to lead the body of Christ toward a closer walk to God and set on faithfully serving within the church community and beyond. Prophetess Sharon possesses many gifts and talents which she believes are God-given and should not be hidden. She is on a mission to fulfill her divine calling. Bringing light to the body of Christ by emphasizing the importance of "LOVE" as the ultimate path to God. Her ministry, "Free In God Ministries," was birthed from her unwavering commitment to the love of Christ.

Prophetess Sharon is known for hosting the *"Woman God Sees Prophetic Encounter Conference"*- annually. These conferences draw people from around the world to free them from ending bondages that hindered them from experiencing Daddy God's love, freedom, and presence. She is active on various platforms, including Facebook, radio broadcasts, and clubhouse, where she ministers the word of God and offers prophetic insights into the lives of God's people.

Prophetess Allen is one of the authors of the book "Heart Check," where she gives her testimony of how she overcame the spirit of rejection. Now her joy and peace come from knowing God is in control of her life. She is faithful in obeying, trusting, delighting, committing, believing, and resting in His every word, and serving Him daily.

Her unshakeable belief is that offering yourself as a living sacrifice to the Lord will profoundly transform your life. In the face of adversity and challenges, Prophetess boldly declares, "No Matter What," reaffirming a commitment to serving God through the empowering presence of the Holy Spirit. Her life and ministry are a testament to her enduring faith and dedication to spreading God's love and message of hope to move from bondage to freedom. Be Free in God!

Dr. Sylvia Mitchell

From Shackles to Strength: The Road to Liberation

In the quiet of the night, as the moon cast its soft glow upon the world, I found myself trapped in a nightmare of my own making. I was ensnared in the cruel clutches of domestic violence, shackled by fear and despair, longing for liberation from the chains that bound my soul.

Growing up, I had always been taught that love was patient and kind, yet the reality of my adult life painted a starkly different picture. Behind closed doors, I endured the torment of verbal and physical abuse, each blow echoing the painful cries of my wounded spirit. I felt like a prisoner in my own home, suffocating beneath the weight of oppression.

But the nightmare did not end there. I was subjected to public humiliation; my private pain was laid bare for all to see. Social media became a battleground, where lies and attacks were hurled at me with merciless precision. I felt like a target, a pawn in someone else's twisted game.

Cut off from family and friends, I was made to believe that I was unworthy of love and support. I was told that it was my fault the marriage was not working and that I was to blame for the violence inflicted upon me.

In the depths of my despair, I turned to the scriptures for solace, seeking refuge in the words of the One who promised to be a stronghold in times of trouble. In Psalm 18:2, I found comfort in the assurance that *"The LORD is my rock, my fortress, and my deliverer; my God is my rock, in whom I take refuge, my shield and the horn of my salvation, my stronghold."*

With newfound courage ignited by faith, I decided to break free from the chains that bound me. It was not an easy journey; the road to freedom was fraught with obstacles and uncertainty. Yet, with each step forward, I felt the comforting presence of the Divine guiding me along the path to liberation.

I fled the residence, seeking refuge in a shelter, but the pull of familiarity and fear drew me back home not once, but twice. However, God, in His infinite mercy, made a way of escape for me by removing my spouse from my presence, allowing me to gather the courage to break free on my own.

Yet, even as I found physical distance from my abuser, the scars of trauma lingered. I lived in constant fear, locking all the doors and windows of my one-bedroom apartment, always looking over my shoulder everywhere I went.

Sleepless nights, limited social activity, and extreme caution became my new normal.

The ordeal continued as I endured public humiliation in a restaurant, cursed out and accused of looking at others, forced to eat in silence with my head down. Additionally, I was threatened with damage to my career and the loss of everything I held dear.

In those dark moments, I was reminded of childhood trauma, the rejection from family members, and the cruel laughter directed at my physical appearance and complexion. But with God's help, I recognized the attack of the enemy, realizing that Satan was trying to pull me off the battlefield with repeat attacks mirroring the same pain.

But God made a way of escape for me, and the devil lost again. Through His grace and strength, I found the courage to break free from the cycle of abuse, reclaim my identity, and embrace a future filled with hope and promise.

And in the process of healing, I learned the transformative power of forgiveness. I chose to forgive my abuser, not excusing the wrongs done to me but releasing the burden of bitterness and resentment from my heart. In Matthew 6: 14-

15, Jesus teaches, *"For if you forgive other people when they sin against you, your Heavenly Father will also forgive you. But if you do not forgive others their sins, your father will not forgive your sins."* Through forgiveness, I experienced the profound grace of God, setting me free from the chains of hatred and paving the way for inner peace and healing.

Moreover, the journey of healing revealed truths that shattered the façade of my abuser's identity. It was a shocking discovery to learn that he was not who he claimed to be--his name, his date of birth, everything was a lie. Yet, with God's grace and the unwavering support of family and friends, I found the strength to move past these deceptions.

God strategically placed spiritual giants in my life who prayed me through the toughest times and encouraged me in His word. Their presence was a beacon of hope in the darkest hours, guiding me towards the light of healing and restoration.

Through every trial and tribulation, I learned that God's love is unending, His grace is boundless, and His strength is made perfect in our weakness. With Him as my refuge and my strength, I have emerged from the shadows of despair into the radiant light of freedom and hope.

Today, I stand as a survivor, no longer defined by the chains of my past but by the triumph of my spirit. Through the grace of God and the strength found within, I have reclaimed my freedom and embraced a new beginning filled with hope and promise.

My journey from darkness to light serves as a testament to the power of faith and resilience, proving that even in the darkest of times, there is always a glimmer of hope. With God as my refuge and my strength, I am empowered to live each day with courage, compassion, and unwavering gratitude for the precious gift of freedom. As I continue this journey, I am reminded of the words in Romans 8:28, *"And we know that in all things God works for the good of those who love him, who have been called according to his purpose."* Indeed, my story stands as a testament to God's faithfulness and the transformative power of His love.

Biography

Dr. Sylvia Mitchell

Pastor - Dr. Sylvia Mitchell is the wife of Apostle Coydell Mitchell. She is the mother of two daughters and has two grandchildren. She has overcome many atrocious obstacles in life. She is a survivor and victor despite the enemy attacks. Her victory of overcoming is nestled in her love for Jesus Christ and her deepest belief that "God is her ALL and ALL." Dr. Mitchell has been a licensed preacher for more than thirty years. She flows under a powerful fivefold gifting: evangelistic, prophetic, preacher, teacher, and apostolic anointing which has caused her to be an effective instrument of spiritual deliverance and breakthrough. Dr. Mitchell is known throughout many regions wherein she has conducted revivals and taught various biblical classes. Her ministry is not only stateside but also international. She is the founder of Women Preachers International and The Grace and Glory Round Table Discussion.

She is a mighty prayer warrior, interceding for others and often engaging in spiritual warfare to facilitate deliverance and breakthrough. She enjoys motivating and inspiring others to walk into their divine destiny. Dr. Mitchell has a passion for single mothers, domestic abuse victims, and children. She is also a published author of two books. She studied theology and has taken many biblical courses throughout the years. She is a dedicated member of her local church, where she works alongside many great leaders. Dr. Mitchell works alongside her husband and together they have formed a new ministry, "New National Victory and Praise Ministries".

A native of Tallahassee, Florida, she is a proud graduate of Florida A&M University, where she obtained a Bachelor of Science degree in Elementary Education. While raising her two daughters as a single mother, she also obtained two Master of Science Degrees in Education and she earned a PhD in Educational Leadership. Professionally, she has worked in the education arena for 27 years as a Teacher, Principal, Vice President of Schools, School Turnaround Specialist, Assistant Superintendent of Teaching & Learning, and Region 4 ESC Chief, and now serves as Superintendent of Schools.

Evangelist Mellissa Berry

My Journey of Transformation

The Butterfly Effect: A Metaphor for Transformation

I often reflect on the process of spiritual transformation as similar to the "butterfly effect." In our sin, we are like caterpillars encased in a dark, heavy cocoon. Traumas and brokenness cause us to hide behind masks, concealing the pain that lies beneath each smile. Too often, we insist, "I'm okay," even when the shadows of our past keep us captive. In surrendering to the awesome power of God, we begin a process of transformation. As we seek deliverance from the secrets that keep us bound, we learn to let go of old desires and sever ties with influences that no longer serve our growth. God's work in us leads to healing—a liberation from the chains of sin and a rebirth into a life of light and freedom.

The Weight of Bondage

My journey was marred by deep, painful experiences. I battled: - Ill-spoken words - spoken over my life - Molestation, sexual assault, perversion - drugs, and promiscuity. One trauma left a permanent mark. When I was around 15 years old, in the summer of 1982 or 1983, I met an older man who seemed kind at first. He showered me with gifts and attention, but behind his gestures lay dark intentions. I was groomed into a relationship that would eventually lead to abuse and exploitation. I lied about his age to my mother and ran away with him, only to be introduced to a world of drugs, violence, and degradation. I was forced into a life on the streets where I encountered pimps, endured beatings, and suffered unspeakable abuse. Amidst this darkness, I clung to prayer, begging God to save me. In a moment of clarity and desperation, I reached out for help and managed to return home safely to Chicago, where my mother waited with open arms. I could have perished in that wilderness, but God intervened and delivered me.

A Process of Divine Deliverance

The scars from those early years of bondage did not vanish overnight. It took years of prayer, counseling, and spiritual deliverance to begin healing. God, in His mercy, washed away the residue of my past with the precious Blood of the Lamb. He began to sculpt my life anew, much like a potter-shaped clay, removing what was no longer needed and revealing the beauty beneath. I learned that being freed from bondage was not just about escaping past hurts—it was about embracing a new identity as a child of God, chosen and cherished. With every step of deliverance, I discovered that God was preparing me for a life filled with purpose, compassion, and boundless grace.

Embracing Freedom and Living in Grace

Today, I live a life transformed. I have experienced firsthand the powerful truth that freedom comes through forgiveness and trust in God. My journey taught me that our past does not define us; rather, it is our surrender to God's healing love that sets us free. I encourage anyone reading my story to know that you are worthy of God's best, no matter your past. The power of the Holy Spirit can transform even the darkest experiences into vibrant testimony—a metamorphosis into the beautiful colors of a butterfly, radiating the fruits of the Spirit.

Anchoring My Soul in Scripture

Throughout my journey, I found strength and guidance in God's Word. These scriptures became my lifeline during times of despair and a beacon of hope as I embraced my freedom:
- *Philippians 4:13* "I can do all things through Christ who

strengthens me." *Psalm 91* - A promise of God's protection.
- *Jeremiah 29:11* - God's plans to prosper us and give us hope.

- *John 8:36* - "So if the Son sets you free, you will be free indeed." - Ephesians *3:20* – The promise of God's power at work within us. - *Psalm 51* – A plea for mercy and renewal.

A Prayer for Healing

My prayer for you is simple: may the healing power of God overtake every area of your life. No matter where you are or what you have endured, know that you matter and that you can be used for His glory. Embrace the freedom that comes with forgiveness and let the light of the Holy Spirit transform your darkness into beauty. Blessings to you on your journey from bondage to freedom. May you taste and see that the Lord is good, now and forever. Amen.

Thank you for taking the time to read my story. I pray that it inspires you to seek the freedom and abundant grace that only God can provide.

Biography

Evangelist Mellissa Berry

My name is Mellissa Jenkins. I am 57 years old and have dedicated over 20 years of my life to nursing. Today, I work as a Medical Assistant, holding various certifications across the field. I have been blessed with three children—although my eldest son is no longer with us—and two wonderful daughters, as well as eight amazing grandsons. My life took a dramatic turn when I gave my life to Jesus Christ in July 2001, setting me on a path of healing and deliverance.

Dr. Tamika Ford

BECOMING ME: My Journey to Freedom

Who are you? Do you know your identity in God? Do you know your value? If not, I suggest you find out. Knowing your identity in Christ is crucial to living in freedom and fulfilling your God-given purpose.

There was a time in my life when I didn't know who I was; I didn't know where I was going or why I was here. Honestly, I thought just showing up at church would provide the answers to these questions - boy, was I wrong!

Growing up, I went to church regularly. My problem was that I knew church, but I didn't know God. I had no personal relationship with Him. See, if you don't have a personal relationship with God - you're just operating in religion. It's imperative that we establish a relationship with Him if we are to fulfill our divine purpose. During my teenage years, I didn't realize that God's ultimate desire was to have a relationship with me. As a result, I just became a regular "churchgoer" without any personal knowledge of Him. At that time, I wasn't a seeker, so I didn't have any encounters with Him.

TROUBLE STARTED

When I was born, my mother was only fifteen years old - a teen mom. She later became addicted to drugs and the street life for several years. Because my mom could not take care of me, my grandmother stepped in and raised me. Even though I didn't grow up in the best environment, my grandmother did her best with what she knew. In my younger years, my grandmother was a preacher; she was the one who introduced me to church. Despite her limited resources, she made sure that I had the basic necessities.

My problems started when I was around fifteen (15) years old in high school. It was then that I began to experiment with drinking, smoking cigarettes, and using marijuana. Now, I continued to attend class every day; therefore, I had everything under control – or so I thought. I was deceived big time. As I look back now, I see how the enemy deceives you into believing that you have sin under control - and you're just having a little fun with no harm done. It seems all good until it isn't.

After school, I had a part-time job during my senior year. That's how I supported my unhealthy habits. One day after work, I decided to go joyriding with some friends. The police pulled us over and searched all of us. I forgot I had marijuana in my apron, so guess what - the police found it and I went to jail that night for possession of marijuana. After being jailed for two days, my mom bailed me out. It was an awful experience.

In court, the judge placed me on unsupervised probation for six months. In six months, the judge instructed me to finish my senior year and bring proof of my diploma to court. He said the offense would be removed from my record if I graduated and presented him with my diploma. So that's what I did. The judge showed me grace even though I didn't know it at the time.

COLLEGE YEARS

After being arrested, receiving probation, feeling shame and embarrassment, you'd think I'd have learned my lesson, right? Sadly, I didn't. When I went to college, I continued those destructive habits and even adopted a few new ones. I stepped it up a notch.

I was constantly partying - drinking, smoking marijuana, gambling, snorting cocaine, popping pills - abusing pain medicine, and fornicating. As I indulged in my lusts and desires, I continued to lose myself. However, I was having fun - or so I thought. Fun turned into a habit, habits turned into addictions, and my addictions became my bondage.

Now it was no longer fun. My unhealthy habits and addictions had taken hold of me. I was in bondage. I had become a slave to my ungodly lusts and pleasures. According to the Bible, you become a slave to whatever you obey **(Romans 6:16).** By continuing to sin, I became a slave to my corrupt habits. At first, everything seemed fun. That's the deception of temptation. It leads you to believe that you can do whatever you want without consequences.

By this time, I was a functioning addict. My life was a mess. But somehow, through the grace of God, I graduated from college. Even then, God was pursuing me; I just didn't know it. I was blinded by my bondage. God loved me even though I wasn't loving him back. According to **John 4:19**, "We love because He first loved us." He is still pursuing me, but now I am pursuing him back.

Back then, I was so ashamed. I stopped going to church and avoided church people because I was afraid of being judged. I thought I was hiding out. But God saw me. He was there even though I wasn't aware of it. Remember, His love is unconditional. In **Romans 8:38,** it says, "Nothing can separate us from God's love." During my seasons of bondage, I did not have a revelation of God's love. Consequently, I continued to walk in shame, guilt, and condemnation.

GRADUATION

Despite graduating from college, I was still living in bondage. Just before I graduated, I interviewed with a Southern Baptist preacher for a job. To be honest, I thought it was a waste of time. I remember thinking, "He would never hire me." You see, at the time, I had a low opinion of myself. In this period of my life, I was going through a dark time. I was a mess. I battled with feelings of insecurity and a low sense of self- worth. But to my surprise, he hired me. It was truly a divine intervention. Once again, I was experiencing God's grace.

At the age of 22, when I began my career, I was not yet delivered. I was still struggling with addictions and living in bondage. Actually, during the next ten years of my career, I lived in bondage. Drinking excessively, going to bars every evening after work, partying, using drugs, gambling, and abusing prescription pain medication were all part of my lifestyle. Still, I was a functioning addict.

My life was dark and miserable during this time. A part of me hated myself. Often, I felt depressed and suicidal. Checking out was on my mind. I had no desire to live anymore. I felt trapped and hopeless. My life was on autopilot, I was just going through the motions. As far as I knew, my life had no meaning or purpose. At times, I considered quitting the unhealthy habits and addictions, but I didn't know how. I didn't have any willpower, honestly. By this point, the addictions had become a crutch. In order to cope with life, I resented, I self- medicated every day. In my head, I heard voices saying that you will be an addict all your life - just like your mother. At the time, I did not realize I was dealing with generational bondages and curses. These addictions were in my bloodline, and only God's spirit could free me.

My decisions had brought me to a place from which I thought I could never recover. But God. Despite my sinful and dark life, God's grace and mercy covered me in all of my foolishness. Looking back, it could have been much worse. Among other things, I could have lost my career, been in a car wreck due to drunk driving, been jailed for an extensive amount of time, and lord knows what else. God's grace protected me. He had a plan for my life, but I didn't know it. According to **Jeremiah 29:11**, God knows what he has planned for you. His plans are for good and not disaster, to give you a future and a hope. I had no idea I was about to embark on a journey and discover His plan for my life.

IT'S TIME FOR A CHANGE

I was unhappy with who I had become. I remember thinking to myself one day, "There's got to be more to life than this." I started wanting to change my life. I no longer wanted to be in bondage. It was time to let go of all the addictions that kept me bound for the last ten years. I wanted freedom. I remember having visions of myself being clean and free. I wanted so desperately to be that woman of God I saw in my visions. Looking back, the visions were prophetic. God was showing me a picture of my future self. He was working on me.

Although I attempted to quit the destructive habits several times, I was not successful. It didn't occur to me that I couldn't free myself by myself. I needed God's help. So I began to pray and cry out to God, "Please help me. I can't do this by myself." Only God could help free me - no one else could. My pain forced me to seek Him. The truth is, God was already working before I prayed or asked. This reminds me of the scripture that states, "I will answer them before they even call to me. While they are still talking about their needs, I will go ahead and answer their prayers" **(Isaiah 65:24)**

My mother passed away in 2010. In the days following her funeral, a light bulb came on inside me. It was as if scales were falling from my eyes. It was time for a change. I had had enough. I surrendered and began to seek God, read my bible, pray, and communicate more frequently with Him. Every Sunday and Wednesday, I attended church. Honestly, it seemed like I was at the church every time the doors opened. I was hungry and desperate for transformation.

Change did not happen overnight, but I began to see small improvements. I was growing. Every day I was cultivating my relationship with God. I was becoming a new person. I made choices and decisions that positioned me to walk in freedom.

After much seeking and feeding myself the Word of God for a year, I remember hearing a still small voice in my heart saying, "It's time to lay it down permanently. Today is your last day drinking alcohol." I knew I was hearing God's voice instructing me to let it go. So I stopped drinking alcohol that day, September 2011. Initially, it was frightening, but God said, "My grace is sufficient." I had to rely on His strength every day to not purchase alcohol. Even though I was delivered, I had to maintain my freedom every day. My choices and decisions determined whether I would remain free.

Through the power of God, I was able to lay down all my other addictions the following year (2012). God enabled me to take authority over my life and my decisions. Now I am free. My identity is in Christ, and I choose each day to live my life in freedom. It's a decision!

This journey has taught me that all things are possible if you believe. Since I've been free, God led me back to school to earn a Masters and Doctoral degree in Executive Leadership at Louisiana Baptist University & Theological Seminary in 2018. I am the author of six books, an ordained evangelist, a life purpose coach, and the founder of Purpose Academy and Next Level International, a non-profit.

Because God has transformed my life and helped me discover my identity in Him, I have a mandate to help others. Every day, I'm in pursuit of purpose. It is my greatest desire to do the work of the Kingdom. I am passionate about empowering and encouraging others. I desire to help others grow and discover their life's purpose in God.

Now I live for something greater than myself! "My old self has been crucified with Christ. It is no longer I who live, but Christ lives in me" **(Galatians 2:20)**. I am Free in Christ!

Biography

Dr. Tamika Ford

Dr. Tamika Ford is a native of Shreveport, La. who has overcome many obstacles, bondages, and addictions in her life through the power of God. As a devoted Christian, she is living out her life's purpose. Dr. Ford is the author of six books, an empowerment speaker, a preacher, an ordained Evangelist, and a life-purpose coach. She is also the founder of Next Level International, a non-profit and Purpose Academy.

Dr. Ford obtained a Bachelor's degree in Accounting in 2002 from LSU-S. She also holds an Associate of Ministry diploma, a Master's Degree in Psychology and Christian Counseling, and a Doctorate in Executive Leadership from Louisiana Baptist University & Theological Seminary.

Dr. Ford is passionate about empowering and encouraging others to achieve their highest potential. One of her greatest convictions is that everyone has a duty and obligation to discover their true identity and fulfill their God-given purpose while here on earth.

Evangelist Tamekia L. Johnson

Why Not Me?

As I sit and reflect on the journey of my life, I pause to thank my Heavenly Father for allowing me the opportunity to share my story. I hope that through my experiences, I can inspire others to rise above what the world may tell them they cannot become. I also want to express my deep gratitude to my late grandmother, Malinda Washington, whose love and prayers continue to cover and protect our family from above. Her legacy continues to have a lasting impact, encouraging us to achieve even greater things.

I am forever grateful to my parents, Pastor Charles and Shirley Johnson, for always making sure that God remained the center of my life. Their wisdom and guidance have been the foundation upon which I stand today. And to my beloved son, Romario Edward Johnson – thank you for teaching me how to love unconditionally. You are my inspiration, the reason I continue to persevere, and the reason I strive to set an example of resilience.

Growing up, you never really consider the challenges that life will bring. As a child, you're simply focused on living in the moment – playing, exploring, and enjoying life's simple joys. The idea that life would present adversities or heartbreaks is not something you think about. But as you grow, you come to understand that life has its seasons. The person I see in the mirror today is the result of a journey that God has carefully orchestrated for me.

I come from a time I often call the "good old days," a time of innocence where I was untouched by the difficulties of the world. But at a young age, my life was abruptly changed by painful experiences that affected me deeply. For years, I struggled to block out the emotional wounds that I couldn't understand. I often asked, "Why me, God?" These experiences took something from me, and though I didn't have the words to explain it at the time, I carried the weight of it for years.

During my childhood, I began to experience vivid dreams and unsettling visions that confused me. I didn't fully understand what was happening, but as I grew older, I realized that there are both physical and spiritual battles in life. The trauma I had faced affected me in ways I couldn't comprehend. By the time I was in my early teens, I had begun to face challenges that no child should have to confront, and I struggled with feelings of confusion and self-doubt.

At 18, I found myself in a difficult situation that nearly caused me to lose everything. I was fortunate to have a supportive family who helped me through those dark days. I had moments of despair, but my family's love and faith kept me grounded. One of the most pivotal moments came when I attended church with my family and received a word of healing from my pastor. His message gave me the strength to move forward and trust that God had a plan for me, even when I couldn't see it at the time.

Through the challenges I faced, I learned that when you're at your lowest point, you will encounter either genuine people or those with selfish intentions. Unfortunately, I found myself surrounded by people who were not looking out for my best interests. One particular individual tried to take advantage of me and put me in a dangerous situation, but by God's grace, I was protected. That experience taught me the importance of trusting in God and seeking His guidance when I'm faced with difficult choices.

By the time I was 21, I still felt lost and uncertain about my future. But as I continued my work as a hairstylist, I encountered a familiar face from my past. At the time, I didn't recognize the danger of reentering that relationship, but I soon found myself facing even more challenges. Despite these hardships, God's plan for me was still unfolding, and it was through the birth of my son, Romario, that my life truly began to change.

Becoming a mother was the turning point that transformed me. Through my son, I found purpose and strength that I never knew existed. I am proud of the woman I have become, especially as a single mother, and I know that God used my past experiences to mold me into someone capable of standing strong in the face of adversity.

I often reflect on how far I've come and ask myself, "What if I had never gone through the trials I faced? What if life hadn't tried to break me?" But now, instead of asking "Why me?" I ask, "Why not me?" Every trial, every challenge, and every heartbreak were part of God's plan to shape me into the woman I am today.

And now, I stand as a testimony that no matter what life brings, you can rise above it. God's grace and mercy have been my guiding lights, and I'm here to share my story of perseverance, hope, and strength.

Biography

Evangelist Tamekia L. Johnson

Tamekia Johnson, a Shreveport, Louisiana native, has woven a vibrant tapestry of creativity, compassion, and purpose over her impressive career spanning nearly three decades. After moving to her current location in 2007, Tamekia dedicated over 25 years of her life to the beauty industry as a skilled hair stylist, developing a loyal clientele and creating a welcoming atmosphere for all who walked through her doors. Her passion for empowering others shines through in every aspect of her work, transforming not just appearances but also lives.

A proud mother to a 23-year-old son, Tamekia understands the importance of nurturing the next generation. Her commitment to personal and community growth led her to obtain her Ministry license in 2012, further deepening her desire to serve and uplift those around her through spiritual outreach and support. Tamekia's dedication to mental health and well-being culminated in 2020 when she completed her certification with the National Association of Christian

Counselors under the mentorship of Dr. Alice Millsap. This certification has equipped her with the tools to provide guidance and support to individuals seeking help during difficult times.

In March 2020, amid significant global challenges, Tamekia courageously launched the Ruth and Naomi Mentoring and Leadership Program for girls. Inspired by the biblical figures of Ruth and Naomi, this initiative aims to empower young women through mentorship, leadership training, and personal development. Her program fosters a supportive environment where girls can build confidence, develop essential life skills, and cultivate meaningful relationships wherever they go in life.

Tamekia Johnson embodies the spirit of resilience, compassion, and leadership. As she continues her journey, her mission remains clear: to inspire, empower, and nurture those around her, fostering a community grounded in support, faith, and positive growth. She is a true inspiration to young ladies.

48

Evangelist Katrice "KAT" Jones

BECOMING EVEN UNDER PRESSURE

The journey to life is knowing who you are and where you come from. I am Evangelist Katrice Jones, born and raised in Lafayette, Louisiana. For as far as I can remember, life was consistent with family and loved ones. Although growing up I spent a lot of time with my grandparents every summer, even after we moved to Houston, Texas when I was around the age of 4, but because both of my parents worked full-time jobs, the summertime was always spent in Louisiana. I recall riding there, bags packed, fried chicken, and white bread for the journey. We would arrive at my grandmother's house and a pot of Gumbo and Boudin was hot and ready. My grandmother would be so excited, she would time us and she knew how long it would take us to arrive because she knew that my dad would only make one stop; she would be in the driveway right on time to greet us! We would eat, and listen to the conversations in French, not knowing quite what they were talking about but the more I listened, the more I understood who or what they were talking about. I would go to work with my grandmother, she worked at a girls' residential home as their "Cook" Oh, did those girls eat well? Most of the teen girls there were there because they had discipline or behavior issues, but they would listen to my grandmother and do whatever she instructed them to do. I thought it was amazing because she had a way with teens.

Our Sundays would be spent at church, and then after lunch, we would take a ride with my grandfather to relatives' houses and our last stop would always be at Borden's Ice Cream Shop for ice cream. I enjoyed being in Louisiana, I belonged there. As the years progressed and I got older, I soon realized that my dad was not my biological dad. Whenever my sister would get mad at me, she would tell me that I was adopted, which I knew was not the truth but what I did not know was that my daddy was not my real dad. She would tell me that my mother found me on the doorstep, and she decided to keep me. As cruel as this sounds, it never affected me in a negative way. I soon found out what my dad's name was, and I was allowed to meet him one time in Louisiana which is where he lived. I recall being 6 years old at the oldest, but I never got a chance to see him anymore after that because the only dad that I knew was not okay with the meeting, so it was never brought up again. Life moved on, and I did not think that it would be important for me to even try to locate or build a relationship because I felt that it would be like betrayal to the dad who raised me. Even when he passed away, I did not even think about finding or even asking my mother about my biological dad. It was an out-of-sight, out-of-mind type of mindset. Mom passed away, and I never got to ask questions about where I truly came from.

I now understand how important it is to know where you come from, not only the state in which you were born, but your family tree because I do not know if I have siblings, nor have I ever met my grandparents on my father's side, nor any other family members; I just moved on with the family that I knew with the dad that raised me.

Throughout the years, I learned that some of the choices that I made, seeking attention to be perfect in High School, desiring to be loved by the wrong individuals, and being a people pleaser could have been a result of the lost connection with my father. I grew up quickly because I was a mom the year after high school, a healthy premature baby came into this world weighing 1 pound and 14 oz. at 7 months, unwed, so I did not have much time to redo anything, I then began focusing on being a mother and working to provide for her. Although my life was not put on hold, my focus immediately shifted.

In life, sometimes you do not have much time to redo things, you just pick up where you left off, which is what I did. Later married her father, divorced, and went through the process of being a single mom, balancing work-life-play.

Born and raised in the Catholic faith, I realized that another shift needed to happen in my life, so I left that religion, and became Baptist, as well as my daughter when she turned 4 years old. This is where I understood who God was and who Jesus was. There I was able to study the Bible and apply it to my life. I was able to serve in the Ministry there for 24 years faithfully. I met my 2nd husband there and after we separated after 18 years of marriage, we divorced. Embarrassed and ashamed, that this was another shift to a new church home because the Lord instructed me to move on and that move allowed me to get deeper into the word of God, and my purpose for being created.

I did not understand it then but as time passed and I continued to grow in Ministry, it became clear to me that God needed me in a different place, a place where there were no distractions, a place where it was fresh, around people that I did not know, and it was all about Worship. Because of my obedience, God began to speak to me in a way that I knew that it was him and only him who was talking to me about what He needed me to do.

Every shift has a purpose and a destiny. Now I am okay with shifting and not remaining comfortable, even when I get comfortable. When I get too comfortable, it allows many distractions to overshadow my goals. There have been many disappointments, heartbreaks, let downs when you give God a YES to what he needs you to do in the Kingdom.

Although there have been many proud successes in my life, there continues to be separation and isolation when God gives an assignment and sometimes it disconnects you from people that you love who do not love you. People who are okay with not supporting who you are now, that person that they once knew to be overly outspoken, loud, and angry about the sun being out. I had to recently learn, that no matter what it feels like, operate on facts and not feelings. When we are in our feelings, we do not make wise decisions, but when we are aware of the facts, we understand that the truth of a situation allows us to make the best decision that concerns our lives.

The pressure of "Becoming" can be heavy when you are being obedient to God, it no longer becomes your way, but God's way. Once I hit the golden age, life has gotten faster, and I realized that whatever I am going to do, I must do it now.

There have been many doors closed, but more have opened for me; new rooms, new regions, and new relationships! Prayers and Prayer requests have shifted. Life has a different meaning at 50 plus 1, and I have not accomplished everything yet, every day is a new day to do a new thing! I am grinding goals and reminding myself that, this is not the end, keep going,

Family, and even some friends, have left me at the most vulnerable times in my life, but who God removes, he also replaces. The enemy will use that closest to you to make you feel as though you are alone in this Season, or that you are not enough, but I am reminded that I am more than enough, I can do all things through Christ who gives me strength.

I am still becoming my best potential and I love it here. This is elevation season for me, it is now happening for me and when all hell is breaking loose, I am reassured that God is moving in my favor, even now. My Faith will not let me fail.

To the person that is questioning, why am I here and what am I really doing? Know that if you are feeling the pressures of life, it simply means God is not done.

The power of GOD overshadows what makes us uncomfortable, and the Holy Spirit guides us along the way. As I speak positive affirmations into my life, and to others, it is a sweet whisper that God is speaking directly to me, through me.

From workplace discrimination and turn downs, the favor on your life will cause many disappointments, to get to the promise of what GOD has promised. Understanding that every closed door, there is an opened one. Far beyond eyes can see, there is a plan and a purpose for such a time as this, where GOD is working it all out for your story, and His Glory!

Loving God beyond seeing Him and trusting Him beyond reach, is a testament to His presence in your life. So, to the one that feels that they are not enough, understand that you are being groomed for more and positioned for it. There will be New rooms, New regions, and New relationships in this Season, if we stay consistent and in pure relationship with the Father. I now understand, what it means to say "God's timing is perfect" It's in the wait, where the Blessings of God are being manifested.

You must know beyond any doubt that you belong, and you belong here! I know now that I belong here.

Evangelist Katrice Jones

Biography

Evangelist Katrice KAT Jones

Board Certified Christian Counselor | Life Coach | Mentor | Mental Health Specialist Born and raised in Lafayette, Louisiana, Katrice accepted the Lord at an early age as a Catholic, later Baptist, and was baptized in 1992 under the leadership of the late Pastor Claude A. Berry. In 2015, joined The Lighthouse Church of Houston under the Leadership of Pastor Keion D. Henderson, serving on the Greeters Committee, The Lighthouse University, as well as a member of The Lighthouse Life Skills Group. Active Member of the Lighthouse Intercessors & Prayer Team Partners. Katrice is a graduate of Forest Brook Senior High School where she earned her Diploma in 1990, and also attended Houston Community College with a degree in Business Administration in 1996.

In the summer of 2017, I earned my **Board Certified Christian Counselor** Certification from TEB Seminary & Bible Study Methods Certification under the leadership of Professor Dr. Derek Hunt in Pearland, Texas. Since gaining this certification, I have accepted the Evangelical Ministry, life has changed in so many GREAT ways and I have been able to help so many people change their lives through Christian Evangelism, Street Ministry, and Christian Counseling. For 3 plus years, actively Ministering in the Prison Ministry, to 350 men at the Jester 3 Unit in Richmond, Texas, and provide commissary to those incarcerated.

In January 2019, where I was **Co-Host** on the radio station. We are LIVE every Saturday night on **Gospel Radio Nation** in Houston, Texas. We have guests of all nationalities who have amazing testimonies, inspirational journeys, and life skills that will help others pursue their dreams in a Godly atmosphere. Our quote is always "Your Secret is Safe in the Room, The Situation Room!"

Evangelist KAT had the opportunity to do live interviews at the **2019 43rd Annual Gospel Stellar Awards** in Las Vegas, Nevada on the **Red Carpet.** This was a great opportunity for our radio show and had the opportunity to interview some amazing Gospel Artists, Yolanda Adams, Kirk Franklin, Brian Courtney Wilson, and many others.

Employed in the Healthcare field in the Woodlands, TX, where I am a **Patient Care Advocate** in the Business|Medical Finance Office, here I can continue to share the word of God in sometimes not-so-pleasant areas, to be an inspiration to others even amid their circumstances of illness; God is still good and is a healer! I have received various **Patient Care Tulip Awards** and **the 2023 Employee of the Year Nominee** with Memorial Hermann Hospital Woodlands Medical Center. I currently serve on the **Club Lilac Committee**, where we provide Spiritual & Encouragement Support to all of the Medical Team at the campus, and a member of the Partners in Caring Committee, and here we too support all employees with Employee Engagement. A **Certified Mental Health Specialist.**

August 2023 I was chosen as a Mentor & Life Coach for The Lighthouse Church **"HerSayToo" Mentorship Program** under the founder and Leader **First Lady Shaunie O'Neil-Henderson** where we mentor 50 High School Teens, equipping them with life skills, leadership, etiquette, and goal driven principles with Biblical support. Delivered the

Commencement Speech for their 1ˢᵗ Graduation in May 2024.

Honored to be the 2024 The President's Lifetime Achievement Awards – Houston Chapter, Guest Speaker!

My goal is to open a Multi-purpose Counseling Facility here in the City of Houston, geared towards Family & Individual Counseling Services and a Re-Entry Program Facility for inmates, to regain entry services in all areas of life while equipping families with a Healthy Life based on Biblical Principles.

Apostle Michelle Cardwell

The VOICE

The dictionary defines bondage as slavery or involuntary servitude, or the state of being bound by or subjected to some external power or control. The Greek word "douleia," meaning bondage, represents the power of physical corruption in opposition to the freedom of life. For a long time, I didn't realize I was living in bondage. It wasn't chains or imprisonment that held me captive but something deeper and less visible. God revealed this to me when I began to write this piece: "Your voice is in bondage." That realization cut through my heart, awakening me to the silent chains I had carried for years.

Romans 8:21 says, "The creation itself will be set free from its bondage to corruption and obtain the freedom of the glory of the children of God." Bondage is not always physical; it's often the invisible constraints of fear, doubt, and silence that hold us back. Bondage is the power of fear in contrast to the confidence of faith, as described in Romans 8:15 and Hebrews 2:15. For me, it was also the bondage of silence— a silence I had internalized as normal. I believed it was just the way things were, not recognizing it as an obstacle God wanted to overcome in me.

Have you ever had an opinion, joined a conversation, and felt invisible as others spoke over you? That was my experience. I would contribute, only to hear my words echoed by someone else, who would then receive the credit. When I tried to say, "That was my thought," I'd hear dismissive responses: "I didn't hear you" or "You didn't say that." My parents often reinforced this dynamic, reminding us that children should be "seen and not heard."

That's how I lived my life: unseen and unheard. I occupied the shadows, carrying the illusion that what I had to say didn't matter. I wore a mask of pretend victory, but my silence was a constant reminder of pain and sorrow. I didn't understand why others dismissed me or why my words seemed to evaporate into nothingness. It took years to recognize that God had been shaping me for a purpose—to use my voice, not as I had imagined, but in ways that aligned with His calling.

The voice is more than sound or speech; it's an expression of truth. The Bible describes the voice as conveying divine truth. Revelation 1:15 says, "The voice of the Son of Man was like the sound of many waters." My voice, however, was muzzled by years of rejection, hurt, and fear. Yet, through this silence, God was teaching me a profound lesson: my words carry power—power to build, heal, and speak life into others.

Growing up, I rarely joined conversations with peers or family members. Their responses were often dismissive: "That's not right" or "We're not talking to you." I retreated into silence, and that silence spilled into other areas of my life—my jobs, friendships, and even moments of personal reflection. My only real conversations were with my mother. She valued my thoughts and encouraged me to think critically, often asking for my opinions or help. Even now, despite her dementia, she proudly refers to me as "My Smart One."

Her validation was a rare beacon in an otherwise dismissive world, but it wasn't enough to break the chains of doubt. My default responses became vague and indifferent: "I don't know," "Maybe," or "If you want to." These phrases protected me from further rejection but also buried my confidence deeper.

It wasn't until the onset of the COVID-19 pandemic that I began to see the purpose in my silence. God revealed that my years of suppression were training—preparation for the calling He had placed on my life. But by then, I was so accustomed to hiding my voice that I didn't know how to break free. When people asked for my opinion, I would tremble, stumbling over my words, praying, "Lord, you did not give me the spirit of fear," yet still feeling overwhelmed.

One pivotal moment came during a women's conference focused on embracing God's calling. When handed the microphone to share my experience, I hesitated. My heart pounded, and fear gripped me, but I spoke. I admitted that I didn't fully understand my calling but declared my commitment to being who God said I was a prophet. That moment marked the beginning of my journey to reclaim my voice.

Looking back, I realize I've been living out my prophetic calling all my life. Whether offering advice to friends, comforting young girls, or sharing wisdom with coworkers, I had been using my voice to build others up. I didn't recognize it as a divine gift because I sought validation from people instead of God. When others dismissed me, I questioned my worth. But God's plan was never contingent on their approval. Breaking free from this bondage has been a process. Even now, there are moments when I want to retreat into the familiar shell of silence. But God reminds me that my voice matters. Sometimes, He even tells me to hold back, not because my words lack value, but because the person I'm speaking to isn't ready for that truth. Being a prophet can feel isolating, but it's also a testament to God's protection and purpose for my life.

One of the most profound lessons I've learned is that my voice has the power to impact lives. Years ago, when I left a difficult marriage, I spoke words to my ex-husband that I can't even recall. Years later, he reached out, asking me to take back those words because they had stayed with him, shaping his journey toward repentance and reconciliation with God. Although I couldn't remember what I had said, I apologized and offered him affirming words, acknowledging the blessings that had come from our union, including our beautiful daughter.

Moments like these remind me that when I speak with God's guidance, my words resonate. My opinion matters, even if not everyone is receptive. The freedom to use my voice has transformed not only my life but also the lives of those around me.

Today, as Prophetess Michelle, I walk in the calling God placed on my life. It hasn't been an easy journey, and there are still challenges, but I know that God called me—not man. And because He called me, no one can take this role away. I now understand that my silence was never a sign of weakness; it was a season of preparation. God was teaching me to value my voice and to use it for His glory.

To anyone who feels silenced, unseen, or undervalued, know this: your voice matters. It may take time to find the confidence to speak, but God has a purpose for your words. Trust Him to guide you, and when the time comes, speak boldly. Your voice is a gift, and through it, you can bring life, healing, and hope to those who need it most.

Biography

Apostle Michelle Cardwell

Michelle Cardwell was born and raised in New York City. She's the wife of Eric Cardwell and the mother of Chelsea Nicholson, Christian Cardwell, and son-in-love Tremell Nicholson. What brings her joy is spending time with her grandchildren Layla, Jayden, Tremell, and Kirra. Michelle accepted Christ at the age of 14. She has served on various ministry boards while attending St. John AME in NYC. Before moving to Texas. Michelle joined The Champion Center when moving to Texas. Here she served on the worship team and the hospitality board. Currently a member of Outpouring International Ministries, where she is serving on the leadership team.

Michelle is a quiet, anointed, appointed woman of God, Certified Christian Counselor, Chaplain, and certified with the Women of Valour emergency response team under the leadership of Dr. Allsion Wiley. Her most profound passion is for worship, especially with the Sisters of Song group and intercessor prayer, which keeps her grounded. Michelle was ordained Prophetess and Apostle under the leadership of Bishop Glen Jeffery and Apostle Shanita Jeffery of Outpouring International Ministries.

Currently employed with Lamar Consolidated School Districts at Phelan Elementary as an Administrative Assistant. Here is where she fills her passion for children. Michelle says, "Being able to hug a child and put a smile on their face brings joy." One of Michelle's daily affirmations is, "I know with God all things are possible."

Michell has contributed her writings in two books "Heart Check" compiled by Apostle Shanita Jeffery and "Revivalist" compiled by Dr. Allison Wiley &WOV Inspirational Leaders where she is one of the members.

She is one of the leaders of the Women of Significance Ministry under the leadership of Pastor Gwendolyn Graham and Elder Ida Benjamin. Fulfilling another passion of hers to empower and encourage women. In her spare time, she enjoys reading, knitting, crocheting, and spending time with her family.

Prophetess Sharonda Thomas

HEALED.WHOLE. FREE.

When did I realize I deserved freedom? You mean, when did I realize that I was in bondage? Or, when did I truly wake up to the reality of my situation?

It was when I was kicked out of my comfortable place. It was an excruciating moment—one that felt like I was being torn apart. But looking back, I now know that it was God, in His mercy, who allowed it to happen. John 8:36 KJV says, *"So if the Son sets you free, you will be free indeed."* The truth is, I had unknowingly replaced God with man on the altar of my heart. My loyalty to have someone's approval, much like Peter's when he denied Jesus (Matthew 26:65-79 KJV), overpowered my loyalty to God. Like Martha in Luke 10:38-42 KJV, I was busy with many things but neglected what was most important—sitting at the feet of Jesus. But even in my blindness, God showed up as my Redeemer and my Redemption when I didn't even realize I needed Him to. To fully understand where I am coming from, I need to take you back to where it all began.

Bound by Generational Curses

I was born and raised in a small town in Southeast Texas—Call, TX. My dad's side of the family was large; my grandparents had 18 children. Though my family was deeply rooted in Christ, my childhood was not without pain. By the time I turned 10, my parents divorced, and my mom and I moved to Houston. My father, though physically present, was not intentional about being involved in my life. That absence left a hole in my heart. Psalm 27:10 KJV says, *"Though my father and mother forsake me, the Lord will receive me."*

At the age of five, I was sexually molested. This opened a door to an ongoing cycle of addiction and abuse that followed me into my teenage years. I was raped at fourteen, and the molestation continued off and on until I was eighteen. These experiences made me a victim of the generational curses that had plagued my family for years. I carried that curse—until God set me free. Exodus 20:5-6 KJV warns about generational curses, but Galatians 3:13 KJV reminds us that *"Christ redeemed us from the curse of the law by becoming a curse for us."*

At eighteen, I started attending a church where I felt welcomed and loved. The pastor's family took me in as their own, showing me the love I had longed for. Through them, I learned much about life and the love of Christ. Years went by—I grew up in the church, went to college, got married, gained two bonus sons, lost two beautiful children, and gave birth to three miracle sons. I learned how to lead prophetic worship, preach, and teach the Word. Yet, through all of this, I buried the pain of my past, hiding it from my husband, my mom, and my family. I had developed a habit, through demonic influence, of suppressing my wounds. I wanted my husband to bury the truth just as I had. But no matter how hard I tried to bury my pain; it always found its way to the surface. Luke 8:17 KJV says, *"For there is nothing hidden that will not be disclosed, and nothing concealed that will not be known or brought out into the open."*

Exposure & Breaking Free

When my past was exposed, it caused a major breakdown in my mental health. But it was also the moment I realized how deep in bondage I was. The people I had sacrificed for—the ones I had loved as family—were nowhere to be found when I needed them most. That was the moment when I truly saw my chains. I had created a community around people who would never do for me what I had done for them. I had been loyal—not to God—but to a system that controlled me. Ephesians 6:12 KJV reminds us, *"For we wrestle not against flesh and blood, but against principalities, against powers, against the rulers of the darkness of this world, against spiritual wickedness in high places."*

I left the church—though I feel God kicked me out. Through prayer, counseling, and the love of my true family, I began my healing journey. I grieved. I repented. I realized that I had made an idol out of people's opinions. Isaiah 2:22 KJV says, *"Stop trusting in mere humans, who have but a breath in their nostrils. Why hold them in esteem?"* The truth is, I allowed the bondage to happen. I had replaced my earthly father and family with a pseudo-family. Yes, there was manipulation and control, but I take responsibility for my part. I was desperate for love and placed it in the wrong hands.

Deliverance is a Journey

Deliverance from bondage to freedom looks different for everyone. One thing is certain—it is extremely hard and painful. But Romans 8:28 KJV reminds us, *"And we know that in all things God works for the good of those who love him, who have been called according to his purpose."* I can do hard things. You can do hard things. We can do hard things— because God gives us grace for whatever we face. Thank God for grace. Deliverance is a consistent and persistent journey. The enemy is the accuser (Revelation 12:10 KJV), and his mission is to "steal, kill, and destroy" (John 10:10 KJV). But we must keep fighting. Galatians 6:9 KJV tells us, *"Let us not become weary in doing good, for at the proper time we will reap a harvest if we do not give up."* There is greater ahead. You don't have to wait for your freedom to pay off—it pays off right now!

Give yourself space. Give yourself grace. Learn, grow, and GO!!

Biography

Prophetess Sharonda Thomas

Sharonda Thomas's life is rooted in faith and family. She and her husband, Gerald, have shared a loving marriage and partnership for 20 years. Together they are raising three amazing boys. She has also been blessed to be a part of raising her two bonus sons and now gets the chance to bask in the joy of loving their five grandchildren.

Sharonda has an Associate of Arts and Business degree and is currently pursuing her bachelor's degree in accounting. She is also certified in religious education and counseling

From leading songs in the church choir at the age of four to delivering her first sermon at sixteen, Sharonda's spiritual journey has shaped her into a leader in her community. She is trained in prophetic worship and loves to lead people into God's presence.

She serves as the pastor and co-founder of Kairos Harvest Ministry HUB in Richmond, TX, where she leads alongside

Gerald. Together, they lead "Acts House" worship services, helping equip believers for the end times.

Beyond her ministry, Sharonda is a passionate entrepreneur. She owns and operates Thomas Innovative Solutions where she provides tax preparation and planning services, bookkeeping, business start-up, and creative projects, like graphing and book editing. Sharonda is also gifted in planning events and designs. She uses that gift to help people from all walks of life create memorable events.

Sharonda is passionate about God, her family, community service, and entrepreneurship. She believes in empowering others and building strong, healthy relationships.

Elder Angela Bennett

Overcoming the Fear of Rejection

Rejection is such a powerful spirit. So it thinks!

It is one of the deepest feelings that anyone can experience! Its grip is strangling and it can take you to places like you never will or can imagine.

This is my experience!

Looking back I believe this seed was planted in my spirit as a child. I'm not talking about the ordinary process of being told no! This is part of life. We can't always have a yes kind of day, all the time.

But there is that type of NO when it cuts you to your core! The NO's of being told you're not enough!

Not pretty enough! Not accepted by certain groups! Not fashion-driven! Too fat! Too skinny! Not smart! Too dark! Not spiritual enough! Not gifted! Just not, not, and some more nots!

Unfortunately, this will have a starting point that you will carry around with you forever if you let it!

Oh yes! There is a stopping point! There is healing! You can be delivered from this so-called spirit of rejection! Start telling it No!!!

At one point in my life, I allowed this spirit to pretty much dictate my life! Starting in childhood until my very adult life!

Rejection took control. It controlled my daily life, my thoughts, my relationships, and my job performance!

I felt that I would never be enough! It produces low self-esteem to the fullest!

My hair was never enough! My clothes were never enough! My body shape was never enough! Nothing and everything was never enough!

It made me feel like I was the lowest person on earth! Of course, all of this was my own private hell!

It talked to me constantly! It slept with me every night! It sat at my table and ate with me!

Rejection even made me think that my children were never enough! Not for me but in the eyesight of others! Especially when going around certain family members! Oh yeah, this was bad! Something that I suffered silently! At least I thought but it transferred down to my daughter. It wouldn't have happened if I was healed, delivered, and set free from this spirit! It caused so much stress, anxiety, and fear!

One day after ending a relationship that I thought we had a chance of a future I decided that it was enough!

I can remember picking up my youngest daughter from school and when I entered my house, I self-consciously thought that's it!

I sat at my table and felt this darkness enveloped me! My thoughts were out of control!

Rejection raised its ugly head and was taking me on a journey where I truly wanted to go!

My daughter was playing and now and then she would ask me something! I remember responding but I don't recall how I replied.

I sat there for hours! Making decisions about what I wanted to do! I decided that I was not going to be a mother anymore! I decided I wasn't going back to work or paying any bills! I decided that I didn't want to do anything anymore!

I sat and I sat! I was fully dressed with my shoes on and I was still holding my purse in my hand!

I sat there even when my best friend came and she was trying to hold a conversation with me! Don't remember if I responded to her or not!

What I do remember when I said, that's it, in my spirit!

I got up from the table and headed to my bedroom. My intentions were to get in my bed, fully dressed, and to cover myself with my blankets. My thoughts were to stay there and never get back up!

The darkness was taking me in a deep hole! I could feel it! My thoughts were not on God or praying! I couldn't recall any scriptures! I couldn't feel His presence! I felt NOTHING but darkness!

I sat on my bed just feeling so empty, so hopeless, no strength, just darkness!

I heard the phone ring and I could hear my friend talking! At one point she said that the phone was for me. I didn't respond! I didn't even reach for it!

I could hear her say that I didn't want to talk! She eventually placed the phone on my ear and held it there so I could hear the voice on the other end!

This person, who is her mother, began to talk to me! She began to remind me of who I am in God! She talked and talked and talked!

I think we were on the phone for a long time, I don't know how long.

I listened but I didn't say anything!

After a while, I cleared my throat and a tear dropped!

Whatever noise I made, I heard her say "Ah He has you now, goodbye! I heard that phone click and the dam broke loose!

I cried and I cried until I had no more tears to cry! I got out of my bed, took a shower and I told the devil No!

I shall live and not die, and declare the word of the Lord. Psalm 118:17

I will not be a victim! I'm somebody! I'm the daughter of the most High! I am a survivor!

I decided those chains would not hold me captive again! No more darkness !!!

I trust God!!

One of my favorite scriptures is… Trust in the Lord with all thine heart and lean not to thine own understanding but acknowledge Him and He will direct your path (Psalm 5-7).

Has it been challenging since then? Yes Has the enemy given up on his tactics? No

Did it all change overnight? No, it's been a process!

This happened almost 30 years ago and I can testify that I've never revisited that place again!

God healed and delivered me from this horrible spirit of rejection!

Over the years I've learned to recognize it when it tries to rear its ugliness, but the devil is still a liar!

I've developed a relationship with my Father! A love and intimacy that's real!!!

I thank God that He used my friend's mother in Louisiana to get to me!

She had no idea what I was thinking or going through! I didn't share this with anyone! She didn't ask any questions during the call or even afterward! She just obeyed God and interceded on my behalf!!!

I am eternally grateful!

Rejection led me to the deepest depression I ever felt in my life! A darkness I wish on no one! But God...

Biography

Overseer/Elder Angela Bennett

I heard the call to ministry at the ripe tender age of 23 years young. Like most, it wasn't until the age of 40 did I truly answered that call. I ran from it. Not that I didn't love God wasn't the reason, but I came up in an era in which women ministers were not accepted. It took me a minute to process that one.

I am a native Houstonian and have resided in Rosenberg for approximately 24 years now! I Am the mother of 2 anointed and beautiful daughters, who also work in the Kingdom of God! Prophetess Sharonda Thomas and Prophetess Taylor Bennett. I've been blessed to have a son in love, the one and only, Prophet Gerald Thomas, and the grandmother of 5 grandsons!

I was saved and filled with the Holy Ghost at the age of 23 in Call, Texas in the COGIC doctrine where my leader was the late Elder Horace Simon. I served in Call Community COGIC for 10 years. This was my foundation and still stands a lot in this training today. This is where I was affirmed as an Evangelist.

I later was ordained as an Evangelist in Rosenberg, TX under the leadership of apostle Robert and Dr. Gretchen Cambell of Living Word International Ministries. I have served there for approximately 21 years. Through this ministry, I received bachelor's degrees in theology and religious Counseling.

Prior to this, I joined an apostolic church and was ordained as a pastor under the leadership of the late Apostle Nola King in Tomball, TX.

I currently serve at Outpouring International Ministry located in Richmond, TX under the loving leaders, Bishop Glen and Apostle Shanita Jefferey. I currently serve as an ordained Overseer/Elder/ of the ministries! Under this leadership, I have become a co-author of 2 books, Breakthrough (released in 2022) and Heart Check, which was also released in December. I am the teacher for a prophetic class also under this leadership and the founder of Focus Up Ministries. My saying that God has given me is to Pay Attention and Be Open! God is on the Move!

Min. Katonia Johnson

I Thank God I AM FREE!!

Have you ever heard of these phrases, "Your past does not define your future," "You can do it, "and "Believe in yourself?" Well, we can most certainly agree, that those words are very bold statements, only to those who possess confidence, courage, and resilience. In the past, I would never have allowed such words to enter my mind. Hebrews 10:35-36 says, "Therefore do not throw away your confidence, which has a great reward." By faith, our confidence comes only through Jesus Christ. Hebrews 11:6 says, "It is impossible to please God without faith." Anyone who wants to come to him must believe that God exists and that he rewards those who sincerely seek Him. The closer we are to God, the more fearless we shall become.

Growing up in the 90's as a teenager, life was very complicated for me, only because I didn't love or care for myself as God desired me to. Loving yourself comes with truly loving God first because love begins with God. (1 John 4:19) We love because he first loved us. During that time of my life, my focus was not on God, it was on being a part of the popular (world) where anything and everything goes, such as drinking, smoking, and clubbing. The Bible says in *Romans*

12:2 "Do not be conformed to this world, but be ye transformed by the renewing of your mind, that you may prove what is that good and acceptable and perfect will of God."

Living this lifestyle was never a part of my character, I only did it to socialize and to fit in. Unfortunately, my unwise decisions catapulted me into many wrong and risky directions. At the age of fourteen, my virginity was stripped away by a total stranger, because I decided to go out and get drunk with my so-called friends. Consequently, I was unaware of how I was destroying myself mentally, spiritually, and physically.

After this and many other situations, throughout my younger years, I struggled with low self-esteem, depression, suicidal thoughts, and rejection. These avoidant personality behaviors developed into habits, habits that were used by the enemy as bait to lead me to a path of destruction. As a child, I was unaware of the toxic thoughts and words that were sown into my future. Yes, the enemy used his schemes and tricks to create many self-inflicted wounds. *John 10:10 says, "The thief comes only to steal and kill and destroy."* The enemy had an agenda to steal, kill, and destroy my confidence from day one.

Day by day, I became a prisoner in my mind. When someone is a prisoner in their mind, it can seriously affect their ability to make positive decisions and live a happy fulfilling life.

In the past, I was in a dark place trying to find myself, I was looking for love and acceptance from all the wrong people. My mind was filled with so much negativity, fear, rejection, and depression. Because I experienced a lot of hatred, jealousy, and dishonesty from people, the enemy deceived me into thinking everyone was totally against me. Fear completely took over, but I wasn't afraid to fight physically, which was the most inaccurate way to fight. *Romans 6:12 says "For we do not wrestle against flesh and blood, but against principalities, against powers, against the rulers of the darkness of this age, against spiritual hosts of wickedness in heavenly places."*

Fasting and praying is the most effective way to fight in the spirit realm. Indeed, this is warfare, protecting your peace is warfare, overcoming fear is warfare, and having freedom over your mind is warfare. We own it, we have already won the victory. Freedom is calling today, make a choice, if we resist the devil he will flee, then we will be free. If you find yourself in a low place, stay connected, and put your faith to work, until you come out, come out of depression, come out of stinking thinking, wake up and get out of that bed, open the curtains, go outside and enjoy the morning sun. It's a new day dawning.

Later in my adult life as I began to pray and seek the Lord consistently, my mindset shifted into a Kingdom mindset. Fear, rejection, and depression have left the building. The realization had set in on how much God had already loved and accepted me. *Ephesians 1:3-6 says, "Praise be to the God and Father of our Lord Jesus Christ, who has blessed us in the heavenly realms with every spiritual blessing in Christ."* [4] *"For He chose us in him before the creation of the world to be holy and blameless in his sight. In Love* [5] *"He predestined us for adoption to sonship through Jesus Christ, in accordance with His pleasure and will."* [6] *"To the praise of His glorious grace, which He has freely given us in the One He loves."*

The reflection of this story is: From the beginning God had already chosen and predestined people for His ministry. Life will certainly throw curves and fiery darts, but as long as we know and stand in the confidence of God, we will not be shaken. The transformation will only come once we come to the knowledge of who God is through prayer and his word. Dealing with an identity crisis is nothing more than being a slave who is held in captivity. Therefore, when a person becomes a slave all his rights are taken away and he belongs to his oppressor. Our legal rights were established at the cross, we are already redeemed. As a believer, it is my goal to help the sick recover and bring the brokenhearted to Christ. I pray that you are empowered by this testimony. God bless!!!

Biography

Minister Katonia Johnson

Katonia G. Johnson was born in Shreveport LA. She is the daughter of Aileen and Rufus Kelly. She grew up with three siblings Monica, Kia, and Colvin Germany. Unfortunately, she lost her brother in 2021. She's been married for over 19 years with four children and three beautiful grandchildren. Through her experience, she has learned that the more you seek God the more you will find yourself. Like others in this book, she was inspired to share her story of coming "From Bondage to Freedom" after years of struggling with her identity. When not writing, she loves to sing and write real-life poetry.

Evangelist Vinokia J. Moses

The Release: Walking in Forgiveness

I hated him so bad I could KILL him!!

The thought burned in my mind, wrapping itself around my heart like iron chains. I didn't just feel anger, I was consumed by it. It controlled me, shaped me, and held me prisoner. No matter where I went, no matter what I did, the hatred remained. It whispered in my ear, replaying the past over and over again.

I thought I was holding onto it, but the truth was…. It had me bound. And sad to say, I was only ruining my life because I refused to forgive.

Forgiveness is *"putting aside feelings of resentment toward someone who has committed a wrong, been unfair or hurtful, or otherwise harmed you in some way."*

Unforgiveness is *"a state of being unable or unwilling to forgive someone who has hurt you."*

During the time I was pregnant with my son, I experienced persistent bleeding, constant pain, and frequent trips to the emergency room, which placed me at significant risk for a miscarriage. Every hospital visit brought bleak news, and several doctors warned that my baby might not survive.

My ex-husband, whom I made vows to love, honor, and respect allowed the voice of the enemy to wreak havoc on our marriage right before the delivery of our son, Marcellas A. Baker. And at nine months pregnant, I found myself trapped in a nightmare.

Just 12 days before his arrival, my world shattered completely. My husband - whose presence I once believed would be my strength, put me out at 9 months pregnant!! I had no money, and nowhere to go, so I had to seek shelter by staying with my parents. At that moment, I was overwhelmed by sorrow, confusion, and anger. I found myself longing for the life I had known before his entrance—a life filled with promise, work, and college dreams. Now, I felt abandoned and deeply rejected.

The mounting stress of my crumbling life took a dangerous toll. A few days after being put out of our home, I stopped feeling my baby's movements. A frantic doctor's visit revealed that his heartbeat was gone—a devastating sign of how deeply my anxiety and despair were affecting me. As I lay in bed, feeling hopeless and alone, getting ready to be admitted to the hospital, a miracle happened. My mother, in a desperate attempt to help, called my ex-husband who showed up and appeared at my side against all expectations. The moment he did, my son began to kick vigorously - as if he was waiting for his father to return. That single, incredible moment reversed our course, delaying the hospital admission and renewing a spark of hope.

Labor, however, was no gentle passage. The delivery was excruciating and prolonged - 30 hours of grueling pain with my vital signs going through the roof!! Amid this turmoil, I kept asking, "Why me, Lord?" Despite the loneliness and despair, God's hand was upon us, and I delivered a 7lb 14oz baby boy.

In the aftermath, both my body and mind were shattered. Postpartum depression and overwhelming bitterness engulfed me. I was consumed by so much anger towards my ex-husband—a fury so intense that I even contemplated violence!!! With no financial support or stability, my life spiraled further into darkness.

When my son was six weeks old, I was admitted to a psychiatric hospital, overwhelmed by feelings of worthlessness, trapped in pain, and bound by hatred, rage, and an unforgiving spirit. Depression took a toll on my mind, body, and soul.

From being a career-driven college student to living on welfare and Section 8 housing. From wearing store-bought name-brand clothing to going to Goodwill and Thrift Shops wearing stranger's clothes. My whole world was turned upside down!! I could not shake the fact that my life was on a great path to success until I met him!!! I now see that I was walking in peace and purpose until the enemy used him as a distraction to derail my path. The hatred kept growing and growing. Yet, amidst this bondage, a turning point emerged. I began to see that the cycle of hate was not only destroying me but also affecting my child.

I thank God I was at the right place at the right time - Word of Faith International Ministry. Through the ministry of Dr. Rick V. Layton in Shreveport, La., I learned about the transformative power of forgiveness. I committed myself to church, where worship and God's word gradually began to heal my hardened heart. And one day while I was minding my business, repeatedly, the Lord spoke to me and said, *"Call him and tell him to forgive you."* Initially, I resisted—I haven't wronged him, he wronged me!! I rebelled, feeling that I had been wronged too deeply to offer forgiveness. But eventually, with faith as my guide, I picked up the phone and extended forgiveness to the man who had caused me so much pain.

That decision was both terrifying and liberating. In a profound moment of surrender, I released the heavy burden of vengeance. Forgiveness did not erase the past, but it broke the chains of anger that had bound me for so long. I came to understand that holding onto bitterness only hurt me, and that true freedom comes from letting go.

The transformation continued when, one day, my ex-husband called asking for help—claiming he was hungry and in a desperate situation. Despite the history of neglect and abuse, I chose to show mercy. Inspired by *Proverbs 25:21-22* *"If your enemy is hungry, give him food to eat; if he is thirsty, give him water to drink."*- I forgave him completely, even canceling a staggering $40,000 in child support. Though others deemed my actions irrational, I had discovered that forgiveness is not for the benefit of the offender, but for my own liberation.

Today, I stand as living proof that even in the depths of despair, God's grace can lead us from bondage to freedom. By choosing forgiveness over revenge, I reclaimed my peace, health, and destiny. My journey taught me that while the scars of the past may never fully vanish, they no longer have the power to bind me. In releasing and letting go of hate, I found a freedom that no enemy can ever take away.

Biography

Vinokia J. Moses

Evangelist Vinokia J. Moses was born and raised in Shreveport, LA, where she lived for 30 years before moving to Houston, TX. She is married to Kevin J. Moses Sr., a devoted mother to one child, Prophet Marcellas A. Baker, and a proud grandmother of three. She has a deep love for God and is wholeheartedly devoted to ministry and the calling that is on her life. Evangelist Moses is a proud member of Reaching Out for Souls Ministry under the leadership of her father, Pastor Charles E. Johnson. Endowed with a mantle of prayer, Vinokia is anointed to stand in the gap to intercede on behalf of others. With almost 30 years of experience as a Pediatric Registered Nurse (RN), she brings compassion and resilience to everything she does.

Evangelist Vinokia has overcome many hurdles and challenges that were sent to destroy her life and her destiny. She is a living witness that "If it had not been for the Lord on her side she wouldn't be here." Her ministry was birth out of the struggles and heartaches she experienced as a single mother. Vinokia delights in sharing her powerful testimony of how God transformed her life, and she loves inspiring and encouraging women to persevere and live undefeated, victorious lives. She is very passionate about helping others fulfill their God-given purpose and takes great joy in impacting lives in the Kingdom of God, her community, and around the world.

As the CEO and Founder of Women Undefeated Outreach Ministries and "Warrior Women" (Prayer Ministry) she leads with unwavering determination. She is the author of "The Undefeated Woman," "Single, Satisfied, and Set Apart," 'Moving Forward in Purpose," as well as the author of many other inspiring books for women. Her ministry, "Women Undefeated" is actively engaged in outreach to some of the most vulnerable and overlooked populations. She is proudly associated with the local Women's Shelter and Federal Prison system, where she provides spiritual encouragement, emotional support, and practical resources to help women rebuild their lives with dignity and purpose. She loves to offer hope, biblical guidance, and restoration through regular visits, correspondence, and faith-based programming. Through these partnerships, she is committed to shining the light of Christ in dark places and walking alongside those who are on a journey toward healing, freedom, and renewed identity.

Despite facing numerous challenges, obstacles, and opposition, Vinokia remains determined to fulfill her destiny. One of her daily affirmations is, "I press toward the mark for the prize of the high calling of God in Christ Jesus." In her spare time, she enjoys spending time with her husband, reading, writing, creating digital designs, and playing with her beautiful grandchildren.

Prayer:

Lord, thank You for seeing me, even in my brokenness. I lay down the weight of my past, and I receive the freedom You died to give me. Heal the parts of me I have hidden. Restore what I thought was lost. And help me walk boldly into the woman You created me to be. In Jesus' name, amen.

Final Words

Dear Sister,

If you've made it to this point in the book, I want you to know something deep and true: God sees you. He sees your scars, your silent tears, the strength you didn't know you had, and the chapters of your story that you thought disqualified you from grace.

But here's the truth: you are not disqualified—you are destined.

This book was never just about storytelling. It's about soul healing. It's about breaking chains that have wrapped around your heart for years and reminding you that Jesus came to set you free—completely and eternally.

Maybe you've read these testimonies and thought, "I want that kind of freedom too."

Good news? You can have it. Right here. Right now.

An Invitation to Christ

Jesus is not looking for perfect people. He's looking for surrendered hearts. If you've never accepted Jesus as your Savior—or maybe you have, but you've drifted—this is your moment.

Pray this with me:

Lord Jesus, I come to You just as I am. I believe You died for my sins and rose again so I could live. Forgive me, heal me, and make me whole. I invite You into my heart. Be my Lord, my Savior, and my Deliverer. Help me walk in the freedom You've already paid for. I surrender my past, my pain, and my future to You. In Your name, I pray, amen.

If you prayed that prayer, welcome to the family of God. Heaven is rejoicing—and so am I.

Walk Boldly in Freedom

Freedom is not the absence of problems. It's the presence of God in the middle of your healing process.

So walk tall, woman of God. No longer bowed.

No longer bound.

You are a daughter of the King—restored, renewed, and released.

Let the past be the soil, not the shackle. Let your story speak, not shame you. Let your testimony tear down walls and build up others.

Final Blessing

I bless you with the boldness to speak. With courage to heal. With faith to believe again.

With strength to walk away from anything not meant for you. With joy that bubbles up from the inside and peace that passes all understanding.

With clarity for the next step and grace for the steps you've already taken.

May you rise with new fire.

May you stand in new confidence. May you walk in new freedom.

And may you never forget—you are not just free. You are chosen, called, and covered.

Made in the USA
Monee, IL
11 May 2025

16854844R00066